SERMON OUTLINES ON

Romans

By Marshall W. Hayden

Standard Sermon Starters

Sam E. Stone, Editor

STANDARD
PUBLISHING
Cincinnati, Ohio

The Standard Publishing Company, Cincinnati, Ohio
A division of Standex International Corporation

00 99 98 97 96   5 4 3 2 1

ISBN 0-7847-0526-7

Table of Contents

To Judy

My friend
My wife, for life
Heir with me in the gracious gift of life, for eternity

Introduction

For several years I have enjoyed preaching a series of sermons from Romans in four, five, or six-day revival meetings. This letter that Paul wrote to a church that he had not established seems to work very well when preaching to churches that you have never served. It served as Paul's gospel to Rome. They knew the good news of Jesus, but they did not understand several things about the significance and application of that truth. They needed to stay on-the-grow in Christ, both individually and together as the church. And American churches need to hear many of the same challenges to keep growing, to "have done with lesser things," to be sure of the gospel, and to celebrate the wonder of God's magnificent grace.

The later sermons in any Romans series are great. I have really enjoyed preaching "Rescued" from 4:1-25. It reminds us of the marvelous difference between religion (man reaching up) and Christianity (God reaching down). I have even liked "I'm Gonna Die" from 6:1-11, because it assures us that death is so temporary. And the hallmark of my ministry has been sermons like "A New Suit" from 13:8-14. Letting Christ work a change in us, and growing up in Christ are exciting things for me to watch as that happens all over the church. In my mind are snapshots of spiritual babies, who became teens, and then grew into strapping adults. But I have to admit that I really do not like to preach the earlier sermons in the series. At least four times over the years I have rewritten "Condition? Critical!" I'm still not satisfied with it. That's probably because I just hate to say some the things that you have to say to be true to the gospel, part one. But our need for salvation is the essential first part of the truth about justification, God's grace.

You will notice that in several of the messages there is a picture drawn. That has been done to try to make the truth in the passage more memorable. Even if listeners do not remember a lot of the things we say, they are often able to wrap their minds around a picture. There was not room to include all of the pictures that we have drawn from these passages — like a tombstone that has R.I.P. and your name on it in "I'm Gonna Die." But you might paint some of your own pictures. That would be better, anyway. I hope that these Romans ideas will help you put across the message of an amazing letter.

Marshall Hayden
Worthington, Ohio

Condition? Critical!
Romans 1:18-2:2

Introduction

Imagine that you were in the hospital for tests on your spiritual condition. On the end of the bed they printed a graph like they used to do in the old comic strips. For the good hours the line headed up. For the bad ones it slid down. How would it read? It would probably be pretty erratic.

What about the human race? What does that chart look like? As if we didn't know! An early look at the book of Romans is not a pleasant one. It's a grim scene. Human beings are the critically ill patients.

Paul describes the sick life that loses — sin, godlessness! It is a condition of mind and spirit that becomes apparent in our actions.

I. Godlessness is ignorance (closed eyes) (1:18-20).

A. It is a simple ignoring of the evidence, a self-induced blindness.

B. God has made the truth plain enough, and He has made Himself evident. We will find that ignorance is no defense.

C. That's how sin starts—ignoring reality. "God? What God?"

II. Godlessness is misdirected worship (1:21-23).

A. It is failing to glorify or to give thanks to the Creator.

B. It is bowing before created things.

III. Godlessness is sexual disobedience, novelty, perversion (sins about which these verses are embarrassingly plain) (1:24-27).

A. This is idolatry too. My unmanaged impulses are in charge, rather than God being in charge.

B. Our patient in ICU yells, "Hey, this is fun. I'm free." And we are free to suffer the natural consequences of ignoring God's direction.

C. "Oh, the church has always made such a big deal about sex." That's been because it is a big deal. It is part of our creative partnership with God. It is an identity at the center of our personality. There is a plan for our sexuality.

IV. Godlessness is practicing, endorsing, or ignoring a grand variety of God-hating, self-defeating activities and attitudes (1:28-2:2).

A.   Wickedness recruits partners for hell.

B.   Greed says "Only I really count."

C.   Malice is so envious of others that it has to cut them down to size.

D.   Gossip defies Jesus. He says that we are to speak to another face to face. But gossip whispers to anyone who will listen.

E.   Some children obey themselves, and entertain their peers rather than obeying their parents.

Conclusion

Godlessness is progressive. I begin by failing to listen. Then I misdirect my worship, my honor. Then I move to sins against nature. And then I step into sins against society. It starts inside and works its way out.

God is angry with that. He's angry with the dirtying of His world. And He will, in His time, remove all the dirt. Then He will make a new world. The human race is a critically ill patient, whose only chance for survival (to escape the old world and move into the new one) is to respond to the heroic treatment offered by a patient, loving God. Grace!

A Single Standard
Romans 2:17-24

Introduction

"Do as I say, not as I do!" I wonder if that has ever worked.

Today's picture from Romans focuses on a man in a lawn chair. He is out of breath because of a fifty yard walk from the car. He's 5'8", 302 pounds, with more stomach out of his shirt than in it. He has a five pound tin of chips on one side and a six-pack of Bud-heavy on the other. And he is beginning his lecture on clean living, conditioning, and self-control. (He's a football coach. And around him are is his team of worldbeaters). He is establishing the training rules and announcing the penalties for breaking them. What do you think? Will it work?

Chaucer's *Canterbury Tales* introduced a heroic, poor parson. "First he wrought, and afterward he taught." That's just right!

I. Here is a dangerous tendency that must be recognized (2:17-21a).

A. Some rely on their associations. Self-image is based on possessing the law rather than on obeying it, on ritual instead of on faith, on heritage instead of on commitment.

B. Some are eager to teach, to have others sit up and listen. Paul would challenge the enthusiasm to reform others, and remind us that our main job, and certainly our first job, is to have undergone reformation ourselves.

II. Here is a popular practice that must be changed (2:21b-24).

A. Thieves sometimes have lectured against stealing.
   1. Do I give my employer honest, valuable work?
   2. Do I keep my books, settle my debts, and handle my taxes with care?

B. Adulterers (who are not in control of their eyes and their minds) have railed against adultery.

C. Idolaters (who lavish care on themselves) speak about hating idols.

Conclusion

"Do you dishonor God by breaking the law? God's name is blas-phemed among the Gentiles because of you." Repulsive preachments followed by personal contradiction make us lose credibility. But the crisis comes from the fact that this casts a negative reflection on the truth of God that we have handled so carelessly, and on the Christ of heaven Himself.

But, His name can be honored among our neighbors, when our teaching and our walking march to the same cadence. Our witness to the love, hope, forgiveness, joy, and fulfillment in Christ is our greatest privilege. And it is a grand possibility. God can meet a great human hunger, with you as translator and intercessor.

Level Ground

Romans 3:21-26

Introduction

Notice this crowd of people. Each one is in tan slacks, tan shirt (no pockets), white cotton socks, white canvas shoes. They're all alive. One man entered the dressing room in a Hickey-Freeman business suit, and exited in a tan outfit. Another went in with blue jeans on. One wore a loin cloth. One was dressed in flowered slacks and a silk shirt. They all came out in the tan uniforms. One woman entered the changing area in an outfit that had "tasteful" and "expensive" written all over it. Another had lips and cheeks and eyes colored with an artist's flair. They both came out in tan-on-tan, with the makeup removed. Just themselves now! Rich and poor, black and white and brown and yellow, brilliant and slow, from the technological nineties and from simpler times—tan slacks, tan shirts, white socks, white canvas shoes—all alike. Standing before God on level ground.

I. There is a universal need.

A. All have sinned. All are caught short.

1. Mark-missing has depleted our spiritual resources.
2. The Jews had the law but didn't keep it.
3. Gentiles had general revelation, an orderly and beautiful world. But they didn't listen to what it said about God.

B. Our sins vary. There are soft sins, like a simple allegiance to myself. There are persistent weaknesses. There are sins of purple passion, violent sins. There are filthy sins that leave scars on life. There are protests of "no sin," which may be the greatest test to God's grace. Nothing drew more fire from Jesus than pride.

II. There is a universal promise.

God will be Just. Sin will be punished.

A. There had been a pushing back, a delay in punishment, waiting for God's perfectly designed answer, Jesus.

B. The law had exposed law-breakers; it had clarified violation and responsibility.

C. If there were to be any hope of reunion between God and us, it

would be up to Him. Only He had the necessary power. It would
have to honor His just nature. And it would give evidence of His
mercy.

III. There is a universal offer.

Things can be made right.

A.   The hope comes from God Himself.

B.   It comes to everyone — no distinction, no difference.

IV. There is a universal means.

A.   Christ—by God's grace.

B.   Christ—by His blood.

C.   Christ—through trust in Him.

Conclusion

Where is the boasting (Romans 3:27)? There isn't any. I lay my
accomplishments beside those of Christ. I hear the challenge, "Now
brag." I stand there in a tan outfit, just like everyone else's.

"Forbid it Lord, that I should boast, save in the death of Christ my
God. All the vain things that charm me most, I sacrifice them to His
blood."

—All have sinned.
—All must deal with a just God.
—All have been made an offer.
—All may have the grace, through Christ.

All Guilty

Romans 3:9-24

Introduction

Maybe you have recently read that list of terrible things in the first chapter of Romans that describe the condition of humankind in general. And maybe you have lived a pretty good life, and really find little personal identity with that list. You may feel a little smug.

Then you read chapter two. It doesn't really describe you too well. But there may be some of that in you. Your confidence is shaken a bit.

Then somebody reads this passage. The room gets quiet. "How do you plead?" the judge asks. We know that the judge of heaven and earth has the answer, so why would we pretend?

"Guilty, your honor," we answer. "But the devil made me do it!"

Our advocate, God's Son, quietly says, "Objection, your honor. They were made in your image."

"Sustained," God sighs.

Paul puts together a catalogue of Old Testament quotations that he takes the liberty to paraphrase. The Holy Spirit helps him put these in terms that will communicate with the believing-seeking family in Rome and with us. Maybe they overstate the case for some of us. Maybe they don't.

I. There is no one righteous.

A.   There is no one who is completely just and fair, and then generous on top of that to the degree that is perfectly helpful to another person.

II. There is no one who understands.

A.   So often we do not want to understand—to really inquire of God. It could mean real changes.

B.   And I can see so little, even in my own tight little community. I can't really see inside you.

III. No one seeks God.

A.   "Sure we do," many will say.

B.   But do any of us seek Him to the degree He deserves?

IV. All have turned away . . . and become worthless . . . not even one does good . . . .

A. I might protest, "compared with other people."

B. But, when I compare myself with God's law, and with Jesus, how can I deny that I have turned away?

V. Their throats are open graves.

A. This may be the "good person's sin," playing fast and loose with the whole truth, and with fairness, and with reputations. But the dragon of gossip is a killer. It kills reputations. It kills relationships. It can even kill people. One small-town family was filled with happiness and love in spite of the young mother's poor health since the second child's birth. The village gossip started an untrue rumor about the husband being unfaithful to his wife, and one day she heard the story. Sick and in despair because she believed the gossip she took the lives of her two children, and then her own. When her husband came home that evening, he found the three of them hanging from a basement beam.

B. Charles Swindoll has some pretty good recommendations about the tongue: think first, talk less, start today.

VI. They are swift to shed blood, and to leave ruin and misery .

Conclusion

All of this leaves us terribly uncomfortable (which is exactly the apostle's purpose for spelling it out). Are you finished with your defense now? Your excuses? What are you going to do?

Rescued

Romans 4:1-25

Introduction

Imagine how you would feel if, through idle curiosity and bad judgment, you became hopelessly lost in a cave. The way you entered was blocked by a rock-slide, and at every turn you found a dead end. Just when you were at the brink of despair, you came to a pool of water; and you saw a stream of light coming in from the other side. A way of escape! Yet to get there you must swim underneath the rock wall in the hope of coming up to light and air and safety on the other side.

Paul presents the spiritual reality from which the imaginary picture comes.

I. God offers an undeserved rescue.

A.   Not one of us has ever become so good that God feels compelled to draw us victoriously into heaven.

B.   Yet He has made a way by which my sins can be covered. He will not take account of my sin. He changes my status.

C.   I have created my desperate dilemma. God provides a way out.

II. The rescue that He offers is received by faith.

A.   Faith is trust.

When we were young boys, several of us liked to play the "trust" game. You stood in front of me and fell backward. You kept your body rigid. You trusted that I would put my arms under yours and catch you just before you smashed yourself on the ground. Dangerous game! Boys could have bad judgment or they could have made a mistake. But that "I'm in your hands" approach is exactly the kind of faith in Him that God expects from us. It is reasonable. The Lord God has a wonderful record, and He does not have the fallibility of young boys. But we must still leap into something that we do not see completely.

B.   It is not faith in general that wins life, not faith in everybody and everything. Some faith is foolish trust.

C.   It is faith in God, who has the power to do what He has promised.

D. It is a total faith. Saving faith does not reserve some self-protec-
    tion clause, "just in case this doesn't work."

E. It is a faith that follows through.
    Abraham in hope believed against all hope. He believed God
    stubbornly, when natural laws and rationality opposed the
    promise. The fact was that he was 100 and Sarah was 90. Their
    having a child was a pretty far-fetched notion. But God's word
    meant more to him than experience. Faith won, and good sense
    lost. It was not possible for Abraham and Sarah to have one
    descendent, but their descendants are beyond numbering.

F. Faith acts according to direction and believes that God will bring
    results.
    Abraham and Sarah created a child in love's normal way. It
    was not some unnatural event. God just brought the dead seed
    and the dead womb alive. In trust they acted, and a son was
    born.

III. The believer is rescued to a new place.

A. On the basis of this kind of faith Abraham was called righteous.
    He was set right with God.

B. We can be credited with righteousness, when we accept that
    Christ, God's Son, was delivered up to death for our sins and
    raised to life for our justification.

Conclusion

In the darkness of the hopelessness of sin God has provided a way of
escape. It is unearned. It is quite undeserved. Light unmistakably gives
the promise of freedom and life on the other side of the pool. The
path of escape just has to be taken.

Life is like a rock-slide-sealed cave. We breath for a while, and then we
either trust the swim to light (in the way provided graciously by God),
or we hold on to the supposed safety of our temporary quarters and
die. It so happens that a significant act of resigned faith leads us to
burial in a pool.

Peace on Earth? How?

Romans 5:1-11

Introduction

How in the world can there ever be peace? It's a world where planes are bombed and judges assassinated. Children are molested. Police are ambushed. Gangs control the streets. Drug lords corrupt whole neighborhoods. It's a world of Serbs and Croat and Muslims, of Iran, of Palestine and Israel. Three years ago it was other wars. Next year it will be someone else.

In the realm of subtler warfare watch the employer and the employee, each protecting his back. Watch the husband and the wife, each unwilling to lose the advantage. Hear, "Just leave me alone. Don't get in the way of what I want."

What peace? We identify with the line in the Christmas song, "I Heard the Bells on Christmas Day." "And in despair I bowed my head; there is no peace on earth, I said. For hate is strong and mocks the song of peace on earth, good will to men."

I. There is peace on earth for those who accept the cure and the rule of the One who brings peace.

A. We have peace with God and are justified through faith in Christ. We stand by grace. We have hope. Over and over Paul inserts, in chapters five through eight, *Christ, Christ, Christ, Christ*. It is no less true in 1996. "One way to peace, through the power of the cross."

B. The peace comes from God Himself.
1. It is an unparalleled expression of love.
2. It let justice be carried out and upheld the honor of the law.
3. It was an amazing, shocking love. "While we were yet sinners, Christ died for us."

II. There is peace on earth for those who adopt the way, the manner, the style of the One who brings peace. We are equipped with personal reconciliation and we mirror God's reconciling character.

A. Suffering turns to perseverance.

B. Perseverance is followed by proven character.

C.   And that character strengthens hope.

D.   Add to that 2 Corinthians 5:18, "All this is from God, who reconciled us to Himself through Christ, and gave us the ministry of
reconciliation."
1.   We are peacemakers who present the reconciler.
2.   We are peacemakers who represent the reconciler. We serve
on his behalf with divided people.

Conclusion

There is a gap between us and God, caused by sin. We have been enemies of other people because of the same thing. Christ fills the gap.
Reconciliation through Christ has a divine result. You and I are joined
back with God. And it has a human result. You and I are rejoined with
each other.

Is there another Christian from whom you must not stay separated?
Is reconciliation a word that cries out its importance to you?
Do you affirm Christ Jesus as Lord — God's way to reconciliation?

The Verdict Changed

Romans 5:6-11

Introduction

Have you wondered if real courtrooms are like the ones on TV? Or like the ones in your imagination? Maybe you see yourself standing in front of a judge and hearing the words "You're guilty;" and the gavel crashes down and shakes the whole room.

We're guilty, guilty as sin. There is a debt to be satisfied, a sentence to be served. And we are bankrupt. We have no grounds for appeal. There are no extenuating circumstances. We're guilty. Everyone knows it, including ourselves.

Then that strange picture changes. A young man walks up beside us, and the judge up there on the bench introduces him. "This is my son," he says. "I'm going to send him to the penitentiary so you are free to go."

What an unlikely story! But that's the message of Easter.

I. Notice some words that Paul uses to describe our *plight.*

A.   We are powerless. Picture quicksand.

B.   We are ungodly, darkened in mind, and degraded in life.

C.   We are sinners. Our lives have missed the target.

D.   We deserve God's wrath. We have no trouble understanding that.

E.   We are God's enemies.

Then came "the week." It was a real time, and there was the real man. It was not an accident. It was not an impulse on God's part. It was a plan set from the beginning of time. The King came to town. He presented Himself. Then for a few days he taught the things that would be expected of those who permit the king to take their place (who would be His people, as He would be their sacrifice).

II. Our living will be powerful if it is guided by "the week's" parables of Jesus, as recorded in Matthew!

A.   Use your potential and bear fruit (fig tree, Matthew 21:18-22).

B.   Doing is the important thing, not promises (the two sons,

Matthew 21:28-32).

C. Those of us who live on the owner's property had better accept the owner's son (Matthew 21:33-46).

D. There is a banquet, and you are invited. Just come and wear the right clothes (the clothes that you are given, Matthew 22:1-14).

E. Be a good citizen of your present country, and a good citizen of Heaven (Matthew 22:15-22).

F. Stay ready. Be ready right now, and be ready in case there is a delay (the bridesmaids, Matthew 24:36—25:13).

G. It matters how we treat other people while we wait for Christ (the sheep and the goats, Matthew 25:31-46).

H. Use your talents, your one or two or five. (Don't you think that God is going to be especially irate if He comes and finds a five-talent person who has buried them, Matthew 25:14-30)?

III. Remember Paul's description of the *action*.

A. While we were still powerless, Christ died for us.

B. While we are still sinners, Christ died for us.

C. While we were still enemies, we were reconciled to God through the death of His Son.

   The judge puts on the robes of a higher court, reverses His own just verdict, and sentences His own Son (not just to serve time for us, but) to be executed in our place.

IV. Listen again to the words Paul uses to describe the *result*.

A. We are justified — obligations fulfilled.

B. We are saved.
   1. We are saved for spiritual cleanness.
   2. We are saved from the wrath of God and from the doom that the ungodly have coming later.

C. We are reconciled.
   1. We are changed from enmity to friendship.
   2. The action is on God's part, but needs an acceptance on our part.
   3. When we change our allegiance, God changes the result.

I'm Gonna Die

Romans 6:1-11

Introduction

Years ago in *Sports Illustrated* there was an article about Ken (Hawk) Harrelson (crowd pleaser, fancy dresser, with a tremendous nose). The last sentence quoted him, "Hawk, you're beautiful. Don't ever die." But he will, and his flash has faded already.

Many of us harbor the unspoken illusion of immortality. You older folks will die, and you weaker ones, even you who seem young and vital. But not me. I'm special. We know better in our minds, but many of us order our lives as if we were like author Alfred Lord Tennyson's little brook — "For men may come and men may go, but I go on forever."

We make pathetic efforts to disguise the aging process — surgeries, layers of paint. People want to camouflage the fact that they are growing older.

If you can read the obituary column and say honestly and without bitterness, "One of these days my name is going to be there," you have begun to deal with the illusion.

When the Christian thinks of death, more than one thought should come to mind.

I. The Christian is dead to sin.

A. Sin will not be allowed to take over for any reason.

B. The truth is, Christian, that sin is not the arena of your life any more. When you came to Christ, sin lost control. Now it is a raider, a sniper, troublesome and irritating in its assaults and pretensions against us. But it is not in control.

C. The Christian has said, "Jesus is Lord." Sin and Jesus cannot both be Lord.

II. The Christian has identified with Christ's death.

A. In baptism I am unified with the Son of God. In His death sin and death are crushed.

B. God's "no" to sin that He has uttered on the cross has now also become our "no."

C.   And God's last word is not "no" but "yes." When I am identified in His death, I am also identified in His resurrection.

III. The Christian will die again, but not remain dead.

A.   The one reality that we need to face is the fact that we will die. Unless the Lord returns soon, we will all experience death. And there is a genuine horror in death for those who are separated from God.

B.   But with the Christian, death has no more dominion, no power to hold.

 Picture it this way. A 240 pound eighteen-year-old is on the wrestling mat with a 45 pound pre-schooler on his back. The little fellow may fantasize that he is in control. But he is on top only as long as the young man wants to restrain his strength. Then, very easily, at will he reverses for an easy pin. That's all the power death has any more.

C.   And, all along the way the Christian is alive in Christ.

Conclusion

An 81-year-old Christian with an inoperable lung cancer wrote, "Death is not defeat. It is creative deed. Its dark night is not extinction but the womb of new light and life. I go to my encounter with this ordeal of death with gladness."

I'm Gonna die — for a while.
I'm Gonna live — forever.

The Gift of God is Eternal Life
Romans 6:15-23

Introduction

Ebenezer Scrooge got a look at the past, present, and future. It was pretty frightening. *A Christmas Carol* is a secular tale with some elements of sensitivity and real insight. "I am the ghost of Christmas past," said his partner and mentor in meanness, Jacob Marley. The past made him sweat. Spiriting around through the present he saw the condition of the his trusted employee's family; and he saw how he was viewed in the streets. The present made him think. And in the future he saw the natural result of his present activity. The look at the future made him change.

This scripture takes more than some casual look at past, present, and future. This is the way it must be for the Christian.

I. The Past

A. You were a slave to sin, headed toward death (v. 16).

    1. Such a slide down an inclined plain may seem fun at first. But that illusion will not last.

    2. The consequences become far worse than they seem. The result is much worse than death. The one who remains a slave to sin gains hell, not just a releasing rest, with nothing to follow.

B. You offered the parts of your body to impurity and to an ever-increasing wickedness (v. 19).

    1. Here's a good picture of a slave to sin.

    2. Eyes, mouth, hands, glands, feet, brain are all offered to impurity.

C. You lived free from the control of righteousness (v. 20). You were free from the impulse of conscience toward right conduct.

No wonder non-Christians think differently about so many things — about baby-killing abortions, about homosexuality, about selfishness, about feeling free to pour and poke poisons into their systems, about viewing the filth that spews from television sets, and about disposing of the vulnerable elderly. But why should we think it so strange? They have no God-sense, no real loyalty past self; and they have a thoroughgoing dedication to the temporary. They are free from the control of righteousness.

D. The past was a life without benefit (v. 21).

II. The Present (for the Christian).
A. Now you are a slave to obedience.
1. You are set free from the hold of sin.
2. You are set free from the need to respond to sin's insistent demands for your loyalty.
3. You are invested with a new power of virtue.

B. Now you offer the parts of your body to righteousness, leading to holiness. You agree with the will of God, and grow in a life that pleases Him.

C. You are a slave to God (v. 22).

III. The Future.
A. Eternal life will find us face to face with God. We are presently subject to death. But, when we are in Christ, we only briefly stop there.

B. That eternal life comes as God's free gift, for all who will accept it.

C. That eternal life is in Christ Jesus.

Conclusion
Some of our friends are out there yet in the past. They are rotting, dying. Their choices are sick and sour, but they can hardly see that. They must be exposed to Christ, who can turn the key in their lives and switch them from lostness to salvation, from hopelessness to hope, and from illness to health.

• You can tell them about Him, even as they watch Him at work in you.
• You can love them into the church, where others can join you in the telling and the caring.
• You can expose them to the piercing, powerful word of God, which tells it like it is, about life and eternity.

A Look at the Dump

Romans 7:7-25

Introduction

Some doting mothers and fathers believe that their children are incapable of wrong. When a teacher or a neighbor suggests that son or daughter has done something mean or destructive, mom and dad look through tinted glasses and call the accusers liars. All they can see is sweetness. They're sure that there must be just reason for anything that sissy or junior might have done.

Or we believe ourselves to be that way. "Hey, I'm not so bad. I'm right. All those other people are just trying to rip me up. Get off my case. Straighten them out. They're the ones messed up."

But God pulls off the rose-colored glasses and gives us a look at the real situation.

I. The Law draws a contrast between death and life.

A. The law is not sin, but it is awfully good at pointing out sin.

I thought the symbolic picture of my personal landscape might be a slightly rocky field. But the law shows me that it is the city dump. It interrupts my blissful ignorance, creates a discomfort, in order that I might reach for the opportunity to live.

"Dump" is a better picture than landfill. In 1996 we want to sanitize the way we look at garbage. Garbage isn't garbage, it's, uh, partially used and partially refused material that appears presently and momentarily less desirable.

In the dump are things ragged, rotting, broken, empty, defective. That's me! See the circling birds and the fires and the rats. Smell the decay. Feel underfoot the slime and the ash and the dangerous shards of broken things. Apart from the Savior, that's me.

B. The law shows me my sin.

1. "No other gods" — but we worship ourselves.
2. "No idols" — but we invest hours and energy in possessions.
3. "No taking of the name of God frivolously" but "Oh, God" we say.
4. "Remember the Sabbath" — but we don't rest our bodies or remember our maker.

5. "Honor your parents" — but we ignore them.
6. "Don't murder" — but some of us would do it if we thought we could get by with it.
7. "Don't commit adultery" — but some of us might do that if we thought we could get away with it.
8. "Don't steal" — but we have a whole society that gets better and better at refined theft.
9. "Don't bear false witness" — Ah! But advantage feels so good.
10. "Don't covet" — this seems to be behind all the rest, so Paul uses it to illustrate.

C. The law is holy. Its commandments are holy and righteous and good.

II. Now the law continues to show me that my flesh causes me to stumble on my walk as a Christian.

A. Paul speaks, and we nod agreement. "I don't understand why I do some things that I do."

B. My best intentions don't always win.

C. My mind and my body wage regular battles against each other.

Conclusion

Isn't it grand that salvation does not depend on our stability or on our steam? Thank God for the rescuing Lordship of Jesus Christ. Verse 24 expresses the frustration. The latter part of verse 25 is aware of that strange and terrible ongoing conflict between mind and flesh; but the first part of that verse is the joyous cry of answering hope.

God reclaims the dump. His Son is the means.

I'm Rich

Romans 8:9-17

Introduction

It may seem like a half-cynical, half-comic question, when you first see it on a bumper sticker. "Is there life after birth?" But it's a pretty good question. You don't have to look too carefully to spot any number of people for whom the answer is "no." Their bodies are functioning. They go through several rounds of eating, a little work, numbing a few sensual gratifications, a bit of sleep—plodding through the days, brain thrown in neutral, conscience gagged. Then it's done!

But there's another choice — life after birth. When I am in Christ, guided by His Spirit, there is life and peace, vitality, promise, aim, family.

I. The Holy Spirit gives life to our mortal bodies (v. 11).

A. He gives us real life while those bodies operate.

B. That life doesn't stop when these bodies cease operation. The future is sure. The one who raised Christ guarantees to raise Christ's people.

II. The Holy Spirit also disciplines his clients, to help us live in a manner that befits our destiny (v. 12ff.).

A. We will make our decisions, and we will do our work. The Holy Spirit moves and prompts us.

B. The power is there for fighting temptation, for persisting, for turning the tables on apparent frustration. We have to make use of it.

C. Since we are in Christ we are not under obligation to the flesh. We don't have to come running to satisfy its every beckoning.

   Sarge, in the Beetle Bailey comic strips, takes orders from his stomach. And he seems to be a model for a lot of people. That may illustrate one of the best reasons for fasting. I can illustrate to myself that I don't have to take orders from my stomach. Am I in charge, or is my flesh in charge of me?

D. Discipline is a splendid Christian calling — my self-discipline and my positive cooperation with the Spirit's disciplines. You will remember from chapter five in Galatians that a piece of the fruit that the Holy Spirit is prepared to produce in us is self-control.

III. The Holy Spirit will help our eyesight. He will help us see that we are children of God (v. 15).

A.   We are sons. We have dignity.

B.   We are children. We are dependent.

C.   We are not slaves. So we will live like proper children. We can bask in the love of the family, accept the provisions of the family, and work according to the rules of the family. And the Holy Spirit reminds us, as a good parent does—"Remember who you are!"

IV. The Holy Spirit awakens our joy, by showing us our inheritance (vv. 16, 17).

A.   We have an estate, an endowment.

B.   We have begun to enjoy the downpayment.

C.   And the big chunk of the inheritance is coming later.
   1.   We are heirs of God.
   2.   We are fellow-heirs with Christ.

Conclusion

It's hard to imagine just how wealthy that is. "He owns the cattle on a thousand hills, the wealth in every mine. He is my Father, and they're mine as well."

The Holy Spirit does not lead us like a dog-owner with a leash. He leads like an experienced jungle guide. He is here to show the safe and satisfying way; and if we follow it, we will reach our goal.

Doing What We Can't Do

Romans 8:18-27

Introduction

When I read the comic strips, I have always felt bad for Beetle Bailey. It is not exactly funny the way Sarge pulverizes him. He lies there in a mangled pile, broken and twisted, unrecognizable. In real life someone like that couldn't survive. But with the touch of the artist's pen our hero is whole again. That may be a frivolous way to describe our possibilities with God. A decimated pile of sort-of-humanity like that, whose recovery is not possible, pretty well draws the picture. Then the touch of the Master's hand makes wholeness return.

I. We cannot, of ourselves, get out of this life alive.

A. Something is radically wrong.

B. Human sin spoils everything in creation. Even the support system has suffered.

C. Into this God brings a surprise offer—redemption, life, a new heaven and a new earth.

D. Christians will not only get out of this life alive, but we will get on to things far better.

E. So, with far better things ahead, even if we have some pain to endure in order to stay in tune with Christ, that pain is well worth handling.

II. We can't, of ourselves, get life out of these years.

A. We have fine capacities, but a record of poor achievement.

B. Christians, anticipating a perfect place, now live in a most imperfect one.

C. Struggle and frustration are the typical scenes presently — a groaning world peopled by groaning citizens. We have brought a good deal of it on ourselves. And some of the frustration has been accented by God to illustrate the fact to us that tasting everything here can't bring life.

D. But Jesus, who came in the flesh, broke the hold of flesh; and He makes it possible for the believer to break the old patterns and walk according to the Spirit now too. (8:6—"The mind of sinful man is death, but the mind controlled by the Spirit is life and peace)."

E. We live in the time of "not yet," and we wait patiently and productively, using the time to advance toward the goal.

F. As new creatures we can get life out of this life.

III. We won't, of ourselves, get done all of the divine communication that we require. But God provides for that too, by His Spirit.

A. He puts words to our inexpressible groans.

B. Whatever translation is necessary to make our prayers effective, the Holy Spirit will make. You have had someone else, with a better vocabulary and a quicker mind reword your thoughts so that they are clearer and more on target. That's what the Spirit is ready to do for us. We haven't always done so well. Often we have just groaned. But God has gotten the message.

C. Prayer is essential to us, but our needs go beyond the power of our speech to express them.

Conclusion

Your experience has undoubtedly been like mine. "Thank you, God, for knowing what I mean."
- The Spirit finishes the last sentences after I have gone off to sleep.
- He adds dimensions to a request that I have been too dull to see.
- He takes my good intentions and fleshes them out.
- He prompts me as I pray.
- He helps remind me of the style of the Savior. He gives me strength to say "no" to temptation.
- He helps me see that some prayers are dumb, but that God loves me anyway; and He even urges, "Here is a better request."

Our human-divine relationship is a mystery. It is amazing that God would make such a thing possible. But it is a mystery revealed, through faith. Romans 8:1-4! In Christ, with the Holy Spirit, I can get out of this life alive. I can get life out of these days. I can speak with God, clearly and closely.

God is For Us

Romans 8:28-39

Introduction

Picture this newspaper headline—a box, with a check in it and your name beside it, then the word "elected." It's not like a presidential election, with hundreds of thousands of people who think they would like the position, hundreds of aspirants, dozens of candidates, two or three who slug it out, and one who wins. In this election everyone on earth is a nominee, and anyone who accepts the vote that counts is elected. God casts a vote for each of us. Jesus, His Son, is the form of the vote. If we trust Him to save us, and honor His loving lordship, we are promised the victory. Called! Elected!

How safe do you feel in Christ? We would not want to give comfort to any who are outside Christ. God's promise does not cover unbelievers. But we need to let God's word entirely change the perspective of worried Christians and worried churches.

I. First—A note of reminder (8:33-34).

Each element of the good news affirms our assurance.

A. Christ died and was buried, dragging sin under with Him.

B. He has been raised, overwhelming death.

C. He is ascended, to be our ready friend and representative.

II. Second—A note of assurance (8:31).

A. God is for us, so who is against us that counts?

B. His love is as great as He is.

C. If He justifies us, who will have any success in charging us?

III. Third—a note about our equipment (8:35-39).

A. We have puny pressures against us (trouble, hardship, persecution, famine, nakedness, danger, sword)—puny by comparison with our Equipper and equipment .

B. Nothing can separate us from the love of Christ—not death's crush or life's pressures—nothing from the world of spirits—neither present difficulties nor anything that can come along later.

No created thing can interfere with our rescue by God, the uncreated.

Conclusion

So, what place does worry have in this life of a Christian? "I'm sick from worry," some say. And they are. "The most disintegrating enemy of the human personality," another calls it.

"I know that worry is wicked," a lady said to Marshall Hayden one evening after the message. "But is apprehension the same?" They looked up the word in the dictionary—fear, dread, the expectation of evil, was the definition. "It sounds every bit as bad," he said.

Worries fall into three categories, according to a case study done by some physicians, who determined that it was the number one cause of illness. Forty percent of our worries are about the past. Fifty percent are about the future. Only ten percent are about the present.

- Ninety percent of those that relate to the future will not happen.
- About the past, chant with Paul, "forgetting what is behind . . . ." (Philippians 3:13).
- In the present, remember: "God is for us."

Christ Conquers Today
Romans 8:31-39

Introduction

You may have heard of an old fast-pitch softball team, The King and His Court. It was a four-man team that beat almost every nine-man team they played. We can do better than that. God has a one-man team, that looks like three and plays like a million. The opposition doesn't stand a chance.

The whole team of Divine Power is on the believer's side. Romans 5:5ff says, "The love of *God* is poured out in our hearts through the *Holy Spirit*; because *Christ* died for us; and *God* commends His love because *Christ* died" (paraphrased).

I. Who Can Beat God's Team? Nobody!

You may remember a small kid who was regularly whacked around by a couple of slightly bigger bullies, until one day they came up to him and right beside the little fellow was a towering teenager. "I'd like you fellows to meet my brother." Multiply that by a few thousand times. "If God is for me, who is going to make any headway at bringing me down?"

A. The world will launch some volleys from afar.

B. It will run up with a wild swing, then dash away.

C. But the one who stays in the Father's arms is safe.

II. Who can charge God's people? Nobody!

A. Of course I don't deserve eternal life. But I trust the Son of God with my life, and God has acquitted me. Who is to say He can't?

B. God has elected us in Christ. He has justified the unjust. If the judge Himself has written a decision of release, who in all the world (or under the world) can bring a counter charge that will stick?

C. I have been elected by God. Who can impeach?

III. Who can separate us from Christ's love? Nobody!

A. He is still in touch.

1. He died conquering death. But he was raised. Now He stands at God's side, interceding, conquering today's crises.
2. His conquering power is not diminished by distance, or by time.
3. His interest hasn't waned.

B. He has veto power over all this world can throw. And it will throw plenty. We are in for a fight.
1. Tribulation — pressure, harassment.
2. Distress — the inward pain that is paired with the outward pain brought by narrow, little, self-interested people.
3. Persecution — famine, nakedness, peril.
4. Sword — You've heard of winning the battle but losing the war. That's Satan's plight. He can slice and gouge, wound and dismay. But he can't win the war with us when we are in Christ.

Conclusion

Paul wonders, "Now, have I covered it all? In case I haven't, 'Nor any other thing can separate me from the love of Christ.'" That has to be a smashing blow to the pessimist. How can pessimism be a Christian option?

Christ conquers now. His promised indwelling Spirit enriches and enables our Christian lives. His recorded word strikes fire when heard and when translated into our choices. He answers our cries and intercedes in our behalf with the Father.

Nothing created can short-circuit the power of God revealed in Christ. We are involved in skirmishes. We can be knocked down. But when we have assigned our puny lives to Christ's powerful lordship, there is never any doubt about the outcome. On the cross and from the tomb Christ has won the victory already.

Beautiful Feet

Romans 10:4, 10-15

Introduction

Feet normally are not very attractive. But sometimes they are—when they carry good news.

Today's picture is more sound than sight — footfalls on the front porch. The children come home safe from school or play. My life-partner is home from work or the store. It's a visit from a friend. The neighbor kids are here for their playmates. It's my teenager's date for a special event. There are friends from the church, with encouragements. Occasionally someone comes with a sad report, but most footfalls on the porch are good news.

One of our favorite gospel songs over the years has been, "When we all get to heaven, what a day of rejoicing that will be." It will come to those who have accepted the good news from God. And those who are in heaven will have heard that news from someone. (Isaiah 52:7 — "How beautiful on the mountains are the feet of those who bring good news, who proclaim peace . . . who proclaim salvation . . . who say 'Your God reigns!'").

I. How do I come to be made right, set upright, directed the right way?

A. Not this way (my way).

1. I fail if I seek to establish my own righteousness, as the Israelites tried to do.
2. I fail if I intend to live up to the law on my own.
3. I fail if I try to exercise enough zeal, dedication and grit to bring Christ down from heaven or up from the dead.

B. But this way (His way).

1. I believe in my heart — and repent, with a turned heart. (That's part of believing).
2. I confess with my mouth. Faith is incomplete until it gives audible and visible witness. And Christian baptism, an act of resignation, is a part of confessing.
3. I trust in the Lord and am not put to shame.
4. I call on the name of the Lord (call Him to take control of my destiny).

II. How do I come to call?

A. I believe that Christ is the help that rescues me.

B. I trust that He has the power to do it — to make me right, set me upright, and direct me right.

III. How do I come to believe?

A. I hear of Him, what He has done, what He has said, and what He has been.

B. There is much more that I do not know, but I am in a position to believe because I have heard of Him.

IV. How did I come to hear?

A. I came to hear because of someone's beautiful feet.

B. I am encouraged to listen to "the rest of the story," the message of Jesus, because someone has cared for me in other ways.

A great elder has retrained one minister. Occasional letters from church leaders had not always been good news. It was sometimes a way of passing along complaints or unflattering observations. But this elder wrote often. And it was always good news, warm words, fresh ideas. When the preacher got the letter, he didn't flinch before opening it. He smiled. He listened.

V. How do they come to preach?

A. Someone or several someones have commissioned, reminded, instructed, recruited, and supported the passing along of the message. And they have undergirded the messenger's courage for doing it.

B. Parents, teachers, elders, and partner-Christians have played important roles in sending. But God's commission is the primary one.

C. And God has sent us; human beings. He does not dispatch angels to get out the word of life.

Conclusion

"We have heard the joyful sound, Jesus saves. Spread the tidings all around."

Be Still and Know

Romans 11:33-36

Introduction

Who am I? That's an important question!

Who are you? How are we to relate? Those are important things too.

What about God? What is He like? How do I relate to Him? Those things are most important of all.

If we lift this hymn about God out of this context, which describes the history of His work with His people, it doesn't seem to abuse the message. We can use it to instruct our praise and to remind ourselves of "the way it is" when everything secondary is cut away.

I. God is counsellor. I am not His counsellor (v. 34).

A. Who among us knows forever?

B. Do we understand how the world has been put together, in all of its wonderful complexity and detail, with its phenomenal function?

C. What about the seasons and cycles, systems and energies and atmospheres?

D. How well does anyone understand our amazing bodies and our amazing minds?

Scientists now calculate that if the electronic energy in the hydrogen atoms of our body could be utilized, you could supply all of the electrical needs of a large, highly industrialized country for nearly a week. A DuPont scientist said that the atoms of your body contain a potential energy of more than eleven million kilowatt hours per pound of body weight. By this estimate the average person is worth about eighty-five million dollars. Isn't it remarkable that some folks think that all of this just happened? It came from nothing! There was no purposer, and it has no purpose. This created place, these created things, these created persons are so intricate, so promising. What do you suppose the One behind all this is like?

E. Does any one of us know all of history, everywhere, and the motivations behind the apparent issues of history? Do we know and understand all of the events that are played off the stage?

F. Even now, can any one of us see everything that is going on? Do we know what lies behind the appearances. Do we know what is in the heart of the players? The Christian will be slow to play "authority." We will run from any inclination to give advice to God. We will be anxious to listen to God, to hear His directions, and to adjust to His Spirit.

II. God is the giver. I am not (v. 35).

A. What can I give that isn't His?

B. By His design, with the awesome privilege of a free will, I can give "me." That's all I can give. I can give my respect, my allegiance, my active agreement. He treasures that gift.

C. Then, in His gladness, when I have given that gift, He invests me with eternal life. But that is not any kind of repayment. It's another gift.

Be Still and Know (part 2)

Romans 11:33-36

Introduction

- Who am I?
- Who are you?
- What about God? Who is He? What does He want?

We don't do very well when we answer the "Who am I?" and "Who are you?" questions. There is a bit of a god-complex that rears its head in our minds. "Because of who I am, I must be 'it.' The rest of you are auxiliary. You are support troops for me. I know. You just think you know. You can't be that important, or you would be who I am." In the comic strips, "Calvin" and "Cathy" play out our absurd self-focus.

It is important that we be reminded about our own significance. And it is important that we be reminded of the proper relationship that we have with each other. But, first, we must be sure that we understand who God is and what our proper relationship is with Him.

In another message we looked at two truths about God. In this one we think about three others.

I. God is the wise judge. I am not (v. 33).

A. That He would want us is beyond understanding.

B. And He has been so patient with our rebellion.

C. He has made a way to be just, and to justify.

II. God is the one from whom, through whom, and to whom are all things. That does not describe me (v. 36).

A. He brought the world about. He set it to spinning. He balanced the cycles to support its life. He peopled it with men and women of splendid potential, made "in His image."

B. He still touches His world. He reaches in to answer prayer.

C. And one day the world will come to a halt. The price for my sin, and for yours, will be paid. It will either be extracted from me, or it will be accepted from Christ, who has created a trust to pay the believer's charge. Everything comes from Him, lives by Him, and ends up before Him.

III. God is the one who deserves the glory, forever.

A. We give Him the glory by the way we use His things. And, by the way, the world works very well when we use it His way too.

B. We give Him the glory by our thanks-saying, our personal worship (real, intimate) and our out-loud public expressions.

Conclusion

What do you suppose God thinks of some of our "reasons" for electing not to gather with believers for worship and edification on the first day of the week? "Sunday is the only day I have to sleep in! It's our only family day! It's the only day left for our league. All the others are taken." What about God? Who gives us our sleep and our energies? To him be the glory forever; and some of that includes our public expressions of honor. Do you suppose that we will be able to ignore God in heaven—read our newspapers, take our naps, play our games, relate to each other without relating to Him?

I don't know what a contemporary equivalent would be, but I think that there is a picture in the fourth chapter of Revelation that we can understand, even though kings and thrones are not common in our twenty-first century world. There is a throne in heaven, with someone sitting on it. A rainbow encircles it. Twenty-four little thrones are around it, for the elders, God's people. And four creatures sit around in another circle. God is in the center. Be still! Listen! For those who live, God is in the center of the world. Recognize and honor Him there, by your walk, your words, and your worship.

So!

Romans 12:1-2

Introduction

In just a few days after the biggest American holiday we think "Christmas is over." In many of our towns it's the biggest trash day of the year (paper, boxes, old items now replaced, the already broken new things). Soon the tree goes out. The music and drama are over. Now what? Do we forget about it all for a while?

Of course not! Hopefully, the celebration has jump-started our memories. From God, through God, and to God are all things (Romans 11:36). So!

We owe God!

Worship is what we owe!

What's that?

When we have been part of the church, and have read the Bible, we have some pretty good ideas. Worship is heart-felt singing. It is prayer on our knees, or on our faces, or erect (in honor, with bowed head) and with a sincerity to match. It is quiet searchings of myself in the light of God's will. It is the congregation's hour of song, or engaging God's word, of encouragements, of challenge and thought. Sure!

But sometimes words are not the best way to communicate. You may have heard of the lady who left the church building with an encouraging word for the minister. "You have no idea how much your messages have meant to my husband since he lost his mind." Words may not always say what we mean. Sometimes they are used to cover up what really is. And sometimes wordy folks seem to be trying to convince themselves.

Our worship must be more than words. "Present your bodies as living sacrifices," Paul says, "which is your spiritual act of worship."

I. Do not conform to the pattern of this world.

A. Avoid those things about which the world says "yes" and God's word says "no." It may be that trinity which the world worships, the popular pattern of life which is organized around the moment—a lust for money, sexual lust, and the lust for power.

B. Don't cling to the temporary.

C. This does not mean that we are to be so otherworldly, dreamy, not really here that others think we are odd. We are just not attached to this.

Hans Ruedi Weber, in a book from several years ago called *Salty Christians* says, according to 1 Peter 3:15, "Christians do not begin evangelism by speaking, but the world begins by asking questions. The missionary problem is large today because the world no longer puts questions to the church, while the church usually gives right answers to the questions that have not been asked. In the early centuries of the church, the world asked questions because it was irritated and amazed by Christians' extraordinary community life and service to their fellow-men."

II. Be transformed to a new way of thinking.

A. We have new guidelines, new heroes, a new set of expectations.

B. It becomes evident that we have listened to Jesus.

It is not that we are different just to be different. Our hero is not the boy who stood on a California street corner with a white rat on his shoulder and a gold chain dangling from the rat's neck to the boy's pocket. "What is this," someone asked. "Man, you don't see any other cat with a white rat and a gold chain do you?" he said. "That's what makes me different."

C. We speak words of concern and of good news. They are backed by a thoughtful and faithful life. Transformed!

Conclusion

We owe God!
Worship is what we owe!
What's that?
(I'm a living sacrifice,
not world-conformed, but Christ-transformed).
What's in it for me?

Wrong question! That's not what matters. What's in it for God? That matters. We discover that God's way is good. It is pleasing. It is perfect.

Getting on With Real Living (Personal)

Romans 12:1-8

Introduction

Imagine that I owe you a million dollars. Over the years I have come to you for everything that I need. My parents started it, borrowing for my bottles and booties. When it was time to go the grocery, we came to you for money. I sent you the bills for college and graduate school. You paid for the wedding. You paid the hospital bill when our children were born. When I wanted to take friends to eat and to play golf, I came to you for the money. Clothes . . . furniture . . . automobile . . . gas . . . a nice house. You paid for it all.

Now the bill is big, and it is time to pay. How?

We don't have to think very long to realize that our debt to God is larger than that. Now, what does God, the giver, expect?

The spiritual act of worship that God expects is that we be a living offering.

• We will not be conformed to "now," a slippery, silly world (the soap opera life—fantasies, moral decisions that are switched like a change of clothes).

• We will be transformed (with a walking loyalty to Christ; Jesus is rubbing off on me).

• It starts on the inside, with a renewed mind, in the plotting ground.

I. With sober judgment I think about you.

A. I don't assess you too highly, or too lowly.

B. I see your worth (which there is a tendency to underestimate), your performance (which there is a tendency to overestimate), and your possibilities (which there is a tendency to underestimate).

C. I grasp how you are related to God.

II. With sober judgment I think about us (the body).

A. I don't assess us too highly, or too lowly.

B. We are one body, many members. Each of us has a different function (thank goodness).

C. Each one of us belongs to the others of us. We supply the capacities lacking in the others of us.

D. We have talents to contribute to each other from our natural endowment. We have the ability to develop those. Then, as Christians we have grace-gifts, from the time of our surrender to Christ, when the Holy Spirit came in.

III. With sober judgment I think about myself for us.

A. If I am a speaker, I will do that faithfully.
1. My model is the first-century herald, the prince's friend and announcer. He ran in front of the chariot and told the people what the prince wanted to say.
2. I share God's message, the best I can; not my message.

B. If I am a helper, I will do that with a servant's spirit.
1. I will actively employ my gift.
2. I will not do it grudgingly. Then I would lose the power to comfort and encourage.

C. If I am a teacher, I will put the truth in understandable and appealing terms.

D. If I am an encourager, a prize giver, I will not wait to be stimulated by others. That proactivity is a part of my gift. These "friends" of the church help people run farther, lift more, smile more widely, dig deeper, sleep more soundly, and reach forward with more assurance.

E. If I am an earner-giver, I will do it generously.

F. If I am a leader, I will do it with diligence.

Conclusion

Maybe the spiritual interpretation will be clearer if we picture an energetic and talented basketball team. Some play one position very well. Some can play rather well in more than one place. Some can play with competence wherever they are needed. The aim is a team victory. Play your position, encourage the others, don't interfere, back the others up, and stretch your zone when needed.

A Refrigerator List for Winners

Romans 12:9-21

Introduction

A preacher once told about three kids who made a new club. They had three rules. Nobody acts big. Nobody acts little. Everybody acts medium. Pretty good advice!

In the verses that precede this section of Romans twelve, Paul talks about being living sacrifices, and that it starts inside. We become what we think about (and what we think about ourselves). Now this is part two of being a living sacrifice—living sacrifices living together.

I. Love must be sincere (v. 9).

(This is a Greek word that you know, *anhupocritos*, not hypocritical, not fake.)

A. Love and pretense cannot exist together.

B. It has little to do with sentiment, but a lot to do with determination, commitment, decision.

II. Love hates evil. It clings to good (v. 9).

A. Love is not real if it fails to discriminate between evil and good.

B. If I love you, I won't lead you off toward something ungodly. Standards work. A standardless society does not work. Love clings to good things, and quickly turns away from low things.

III. Love is being a devoted friend (v. 10).

IV. Love honors another above yourself (v. 10).

A. This may be the hardest on the list.

B. To do this I have to have enough sense of my worth as a child of God and as a possession of the Son of God that I don't have to scratch and battle for the upper hand with you.

V. Love is zealous, with spiritual fervor (v. 11).

Right in the middle of this is a spiritual reminder; "serving the Lord." If we need to outdo others, outdo them in devotion to Christ.

VI. Love is joyful (because of hope) (v. 12).

VII. Love is patient in affliction (v. 12).

It holds out. We will not be delivered from all misfortune, but in the midst of misfortune we will be sustained.

VIII. Love is faithful in prayer (v. 12).

We mentioned mother. This one has mother written all over it. One father of adult children prays for his sons and their wives every day. That might get him up to a third of his wife's prayers for them.

IX. Love shares with God's people who are in need (v. 13).

It shares with godless people too, as it can. But God's people are a first priority.

X. Love practices hospitality (v. 13).

Is your house a place where children clamor to come, where missionaries and traveling friends can always find a bed, where a lot of folks in the church family have pulled up under your table, where brothers and sisters can find an ear, a chair, and a prayer?

XI. Love blesses those who persecute (v. 14).

XII. Love rejoices with those who rejoice (v. 15).

It will do that even with those who have achieved a success that you want, but may never enjoy yourself.

XIII. Love mourns with those who mourn (v. 15).

It lifts up part of the pain.

XIV. Love stretches its social range past its comfort zones (v. 16).

Conclusion

Remember, all letter long, Paul reminds us that this is God-guided living that we cannot produce on our own. We need a Savior. We need the Spirit. We may have them.

The Christian and the Human Family
Romans 13:1-7

Introduction

"Everyone must submit himself to the governing authorities."

That's easy for Paul to say. He didn't have to deal with a tax-and-spend President, who doesn't seem to be able to make up his mind. The President smiles nicely but is confused about foreign policy. He gets angry if babies are bombed but calls it "choice" if they are sucked out of a mother's womb. When it comes to godliness in sexuality, he doesn't seem to understand; and his family's ethics seem to be adolescent at best.

That's easy for Paul to say. He doesn't have to deal with a Speaker of the House of Representatives who is unpredictable and explosive, whose heart is so hard that he would let his wife support him through school and dump her.

Paul didn't have to face a Congress that is ready to strip all of the compassion from government. It seems ready to keep "pork" projects for favored districts but grab money from the hands of babies and old people.

It's easy enough for Paul to say. He can be idealistic when he doesn't have to cope with the immoralities of late twentieth century governments.

It wasn't easy for him to say. Think about the cities where he almost got killed. Think about Corinth, the place from which he wrote these things. Think about the Roman empire. It was far worse than our government ever thought about being.

Yet, listen to the way he talks.

I. Submit yourself to the governing authorities.

A.   Willingly, "place yourself under" them.

B.   Anarchy is never of Christ.

C.   To oppose governmental decision sometimes is of God It must be an ungodly decision. I must be willing to accept the consequences of my principled opposition. I may disagree, but I am never immune from any punishment that comes from having broken the law.

II. Do what is right!

A. It must be right by divine definition.

B. Then you make a special, most important contribution to society.

C. The fruit of the spirit is a good place to start—fruit that we are to produce, which demonstrates the Holy Spirit in our lives (Galatians 5:22). "Against these there is no law."

III. Pay your taxes.

A. "But I don't agree with the military-industrial complex. I don't agree with social welfare. I don't agree with those enormous highway expenditures. How could we spend $3.3 million to rearrange High Street? I don't agree with the raises given in our city schools."

B. It doesn't matter whether we agree or not.

C. We live in this country. We are beneficiaries of the heritage, of the bridges built by those who have gone before, and of the "ministry" that government offers now.

D. Pay your taxes, and be scrupulously honest about it

E. Coins are Caesar's business. Let him make the rules about what we do with them. Hearts are God's business—and our attitudes, and our relationships, and eternity. He'll make the rules about what we do with them.

IV. Give honor and respect to those in positions of authority.

A. When they demonstrate their responsibility, cheer.

B. When they think differently from you, listen.

C. Undergird them with prayer.

D. Accept their service with gratitude.

E. Offer your partnership.

Conclusion

Honor and respect! What will that mean?
- What will it mean for me to respect the officials?
- What will it mean for me to respect my family, my parents, my friends, my church leaders? (The way I talk with them, the way I talk about them, the way I pray for them)
- What will it mean for me to respect God?

God's Secular Servants
Romans 13:1-7

Introduction

What's this all about? This is spiritual? Paul, you've jumped the tracks! What does Christianity have to do with politics? Maybe this is one of those questionable Bible passages that some editor slipped in. Or maybe the apostle wasn't thinking.

"Servants of God," Paul says. And the government that he talks about was not like ours—not nearly so just as ours. How can this be?

God, apparently, has different kinds of servants (people who accomplish what he wishes).

I. Some are secular servants. They are ministers of order with an assignment to control this space and this time, which is filled with many interests and many different individuals.

They are to provide temporary peace, in which the life-offer can be made and get a hearing.

A. Government is ordained by God.
   1. Those who fill the offices now are exercising the roles that God has designed.
   2. These officials are to be obeyed by Christians.

B. Order is ordained by God.
   1. He has secular servants in a world that is populated by Christians and non-Christians, by the disciplined and the undisciplined, by the unselfish and by the greedy.
   2. In a world such as ours there must be law and order to restrain chaos. It tutors citizens. It punishes those who would harm others.
   3. If everyone were a perceptive, self-ordered, committed Christian, less law would be needed

C. This system is no threat to those who do right.

D. But be afraid of these servants if you do wrong.

E. Taxes are to be paid in order to provide the livelihood of God's secular servants, who give full time for governing.
   Picture a tax form, with your name signed to it and your check attached. On the form are pictured a policeman, the governor,

and your local member of the Senate. Under their pictures you have written, "respect."

II. Some of us are life-owning servants, who are called to show and tell the mercy of God.

A. Even as we support orderly government, the salvation life is our first concern.

B. They deal with temporary issues, important, but temporary. We wrestle with, present, and represent eternal issues. More important!

C. Of these others we read, "He is God's servant to do you good. He is God's servant, an agent of wrath to bring punishment on the wrongdoer."
   1. We share assignment #1. We applaud and reinforce and form partnerships with those who are doing what is right.
   2. We do not share assignment #2. Government executes punishment on the disorderly. We do not.

D. Government officials watch the actions of others. You and I, first and foremost, must watch our own actions. We are available to others, but we do not judge others.

E. We remember Paul's charge in Romans 12:1. "Offer living sacrifices." What I do with myself is a real spiritual issue.

A New Suit

Romans 13:8-14

Introduction

In the early 1970s there was a best-selling book by B.F. Skinner entitled *Beyond Freedom and Dignity*. This may oversimplify the thesis, but I think that it fairly represents the author's position. You and I are not free. We can claim no dignity for good decisions. Nor are we responsible for what some think are offenses. We are molded by other forces—the make-up with which we were born, and the combination of environmental influences in which we live. And we cannot change.

As Christians we believe otherwise, very strongly. Our will is involved. And God's invitation is involved. He offers the Person and the power for change.

Picture yourself walking into a clothing store. You are in rags, hardly covered. And you have no money. You have come to ask the owner for simple clothes, something about to be discarded. But he gives you a fine new suit, shoes, underwear, shirt, all that you need. And he says, "Now, conduct yourself in a manner that fits the clothes."

God, through Christ, honoring our faith, has given us an undeserved title—"Righteous one." Now, how shall we live in this new clothing, in this new, changed life? In chapters twelve through fourteen of the book of Romans Paul talks about living in these new clothes as a member of the church, as a member of the state, and as a brother/sister to other Christians. Now, in this passage he instructs the Christian in society, in those new clothes, freed from the domination and the hold of sin.

I. Don't play in the mud (13:8-10).

Now there is a reason. Before we came to Christ we didn't see the point. In your family you may have had little boys. They loved to march through the mud-puddles, even when they had orders not to. But as older teen-agers it will have been several years since they wanted to do that. They have found young women, and they now take more pride in their appearance. There is a reason to avoid the mud.

A.   The law simply said, "Don't do it."

B. Now, we are clothed in garments intended for the presence of God. He has given them to me, free and undeserved. And His love has taught me to love. That's the one debt that I shall never intend to discharge.

II. Be wide awake, and watch where you are going (v. 11).

A. Don't switch the frequency that has you on the same wave length with God.

B. Pay attention to, be awake to, the concerns of your inner spirit.

C. The old life wants your energy. The devil wants your energy. Great and rich possibilities call for your energy. Invest it alertly.

III. Stay out of the shadows (vv. 12-14).

A. Trouble waits for those who grope in the dark.

B. The Christian life is open, practiced in light.

C. In that daylight life we provide for the important things.
  1. I meet the physical needs of those who are my privileged responsibility.
  2. I feed mine and I feed myself for a strong, mature spiritual self.
  3. I make no provision for the earth-bound passions.
  4. I put aside the deeds of darkness and put on the armor of light.

Conclusion

Several years ago two couples went to a fine restaurant for a special dinner. They had reservations. But one of the men did not have on a jacket. "I'm sorry," said the headwaiter. "We cannot seat the young man without a coat." Then, after looking them over and deciding that they would be OK, he suggested, "Would you like for me to get you one?" He brought a 42 long to put on a 37 regular body.

There was no admittance without a jacket to that fine place.

More importantly, there is no admittance to God's heaven without new clothes. The old rags that we had dragged through the low spots in the world just won't do. But God will give us new clothes. He will give them to all who will accept them and trust His Son. And they will fit. And we will live in them, gladly, in a way that honors the new garment.

God is First, and You Count

Romans 14:1-19

Introduction

In the closing chapters of Romans Paul tells us, loud and clear, that if we are going to really live we are going to practice brotherhood. If I don't do that, God is going to be an unhappy God, and I am going to be an unhappy person.

- I shall examine, seriously, the matters that affect my conscience, and I am to be true to myself.
- If I am a "strong" Christian, I have figured out what things are important. But I will not tread on another person's conscience. And I will carry more weight, because I can.
- If I am a "weak" Christian, more fragile in my conscience, more concerned about making mistakes, I will not insist that another share my opinion. And I will grow, get stronger, be less frightened, and be less easily injured.

The controlling motive in all Christian conduct is love—a love for God, a love for obeying Him, and a love for His people. "So!" Paul says, "realize some things:"

I. These people are not your servants. They are Christ's (14:4-5).

A. Both of us are guests at His table. Who would be rude enough to criticize another guest at a meal for which you were not the host?

In the paraphrased New Testament, *The Message,* this section reads "Do you have any business crossing people off the guest list or interfering with God's welcome? If there are corrections to be made or manners to be learned, God can handle that without your help."

B. At Sunday worship, we are gathered to express our honor to God. The others to whom we relate are His servants, not ours. That says something about the way we dress; but it also says something about the way we evaluate the way someone else might be dressed. I am not the master to whom another must give account.

II. These things are not your things. They are gifts (14:6-9).

A. Gratitude is my most important posture.

B.   It is a gratitude that is not just felt. It is lived.

C.   It is a gratitude that is to be celebrated, with vigor.
     The Message reads, "If you eat meat, eat it to the glory of God and thank God for the prime rib; if you're a vegetarian, eat vegetables to the glory of God and thank God for the broccoli." For some of us that will be easier to do than it is for George Bush.

III. Criticism is not part of your job description. Faithful personal living is (14:10-13).

A.   Judgment is in God's job description. You and I will both stand before Him, and He will have the last word. Why would I pretend to do God's job?

B.   We have plenty to do taking care of our own lives before God. My intellectual development, my devotional life, giving proper care to the people who are (at least in part) my responsibility, disciplining my thoughts and choices and time uses—these things are more than I will ever get done properly.

IV. Encouragement is a dandy use for your energies (14:17-19).

A.   We have a finite amount of energy. How will we spend it?

B.   It's a pretty good bet that the most successful people you know are encouragers.

Conclusion

Let's put what Paul says in some of our words. "You are really different from each other. Some are stronger, some are weaker. Some are long-timers and some are short-termers. Some are insightful and some are fearful. You wear different things, you eat different things, and you spend time in different ways. You bring to God different kinds of sacrifices. Just remember! Each of you is alive if you have entrusted your life to Christ, even if that trust comes out looking different in each of you. You are not in charge of each other, but your brotherhood really counts. So, make every effort to do what leads to peace and to a mutual building up. Up! I said up!

God is first. And you count!

Pears or Prickle?

Romans 14:13-19 (and Galatians 5:19-23)

Introduction

Funny title! It's because pears are the writer's favorite fruit. And *prickle* is just a word that came to mind. It does mean something with a small, sharp point—a thorn, a spine. OK! That draws the picture. Which kind of life will it be?

The works of the flesh are plain enough. We can see them all around. They can be rather easily identified as animal actions. And, when the flesh runs a life, it is a splintered existence.

When the Holy Spirit runs a life, He produces things (fruit) that nobody wants to make a law against. Paul says something like this. "You're going to like what the Holy Spirit will do with you. You will like yourself better. Other people will enjoy you more. God finds you tasteful."

I. You will be starting with the Spirit.

A. Step one will mean getting the Spirit, claiming Jesus Christ as Lord. Then you recognize the promised Spirit's presence. You consult God's word (inspired by the Spirit) for direction. You make personal covenants with that expression of God in you. You deploy your energies into producing bigger, riper fruit.

B. The Spirit introduces the gifted life to you. In seed form the fruit is planted.

C. You blend these spiritual resources with your human resources and grow. The Spirit will not develop ripe fruit without your cooperation. (God grows the vegetables in your garden; but you fertilize, water, and cultivate).
   1. Watch Paul's love grow riper, his faith and his calling.
   2. Note the mounting joy and the deepening love in some of the saints around you. They are growing up in Christ.

II. You will be living with the Spirit.

(Note two primary characteristics in one who walks with Christ: being filled with the Holy Spirit, and producing fruit that others can see.)

A. The Spirit produces love (14:15).

   1. What kind of love? Mush? Hardly! Romance? Not really! Friendship? That's closer! Unlimited concern and unrestricted good will? Yes!

   2. It's a love that can be present even when friendship is spurned, the senses are repulsed, distance makes touching impossible, messages may not be heard, previous attempts at closeness have resulted in failure, good intentions are misunderstood, and even when hatred blazes from the other side.

   3. It does not tamper with another person's conscience.

   4. It is keenly aware that Christ died to save this other person.

   5. It realizes that no pleasure is so important that it can justify bringing offense and grief to another Christian.

B. The Spirit produces joy (14:17).

   1. This is a first cousin to love.

   2. Genuine joy results from knowing the love of God and from exercising that same spirit.

   3. Joy springs from assurance.

   4. Joy is something that will increase as we grow.

   5. Joy is presently realized in part; but its full expression will be known later.

Conclusion

Our expectation is far greater than this. But the beginnings of our joy (known in Christian living) are a little bit like Mom's having baked a turkey in a bag, and letting you have a juicy pinch. The big slice comes at dinnertime.

I Am My Brother's Keeper

Romans 15:1-6

Introduction

"Do I have to wet-nurse my brother? How do I know where he is? Can't he take care of himself? Do I have to watch him like he watches those silly sheep of his?"

Almost all of us know who asked that question. And it was not one of the heroes of the Bible. In fact, it was a man who didn't seem to do much of anything right—Cain, who was a careless worshipper, an angry son, a murderer, and a rootless wanderer. Knowing his history, we would be safe in listening to his opinion and going the opposite way. Like some other people who have the uncanny ability to be wrong, he had a perspective on life molded by the wrong set of values. When you hear the world's Cains say, "Am I my brother's keeper?" you know quickly where the truth lies. "I am my brother's keeper."

I. What is it that Christ expects me to do?

A. About my lifestyle—If I am a strong Christian, I am to bear with the failings of the weak, rather than please myself (15:1). Your walk with God, your faithfulness to conscience, your personal peace, and there being an atmosphere in which you can grow in Christ are more important than my personal pleasure. So, for your sake (and in the style of Jesus) I will be careful about what I eat and drink, and about how I play and work and speak.

B. About my goal—I will build up my neighbor (15:2).
   1. If is not enough to bear with the weak and edify.
   2. Strength is for service, not for status.
   3. I will cheer another's successes. And at times I will take on myself the pain of their failures. It means that I will stay close enough that I can reach out and give a little bit of steadying when it is needed.

   Sometimes just giving the confidence that comes from knowing you are there is enough. You probably did that when you taught a child to ride a bike. For a while you actually held her up. Then, as she began to learn how to balance herself, you just kept a hand in place, with a light touch, and corrected the beginnings of a fall. Then you ran alongside as she gained confidence in staying upright. Then you stood and watched and cheered. You cleaned up a few cuts and sent her out again. Then you watched her ride off on her own. Competent! Stronger! You helped!

C. About my attitude—Christ expects unity among ourselves as we follow Him (15:5).

II. Why is it that I am to do this?

A. This is the way that Christ, my Lord and my model, acted. He took on Himself the insults that were aimed at others (15:3).

B. God has given you and me encouragement and the capacity for endurance (15:5).

C. Our unity (one heart and one mouth) glorifies God (15:6). Read Acts 2:44-47 again—the experience of the Jerusalem church.
  1. Why our unity? For the honor of God! Our divisions starve our common worship. Because of them we offer God a poorer, thinner, quality of praise.
  2. It is hard to sing glad songs of praise to God through clinched teeth.
  3. Through our unity we get a family, God gets a family, and God gets the glory.

Conclusion

Of all the songs in the book of Revelation, not one is a solo—thousands of angels, the twenty-four elders.

If someone were to ask what we want the church to be, we would be pretty close to right if we said that we wanted it to be a choir. We're anxious to build lives, belonging to Jesus, which harmonize with each other in praise to God.

A Special Love

Romans 15:5-7

Introduction

You have some of the same kind of friends that we do. They live miles and miles away. You see them seldom. Even in earlier years when you were close, you were not together that many times. But you feel a special glow of love for them. You rejoice with their victories and with their family happiness as though it was your own. And their letters say that they feel the same way about you.

Why? Because they love God just as you do. They serve Him with all their strength. They want very much to speak for Christ and to show Him in themselves.

God loves the world. And so shall we. Jesus loved His enemies. And so shall we. But God has a special kind of love that He has reserved for those who respond to His gifts of love. And we will have that kind of love toward those who are kinsmen of ours in life and who will still be kinsmen in eternity.

I. With one heart and one mouth glorify God (15:6).

A. The highest expression of fellowship is to sing as one voice in praise to God, harmonizing.

B. "Be perfectly united in mind and thought" (1 Corinthians 1:10) is a favorite idea of Paul's, put in slightly different words at different times.

At the 1968 North American Christian Convention preacher Jim McKowen said, "The most instinctive Christian act is fellowship."

On a trip to the World Convention in Australia, American travelers were welcomed to Korea with a great sign that said, "Welcome to Christian Brothers from America." They enjoyed happy hospitality at a children's home. And at a Christian college a preacher, who had formerly been a Buddhist priest, sat next to Edwin Hayden and handed him a carefully autographed Korean New Testament that said, "To my American brother."

II. Accept one another as Christ accepted you (15:7).

A. How is that? As perfect, flawless? Of course not! When we have trusted Him, He accepts us as forgiven, and as having promise.

B. We are called to accept being accepted, even though we are unacceptable.

C. We accept one another though we may see some things in the other that are unacceptable. Karl Ketcherside used to be chided for consorting with brethren in error, and he always replied, "That's the only kind of brethren I have."

D. Christian love transcends differences and will not allow them to divide.

Conclusion

One bright word stands out in the gospel of Christ, "For God so loved the world that He gave" (John 3:16). "This is love: not that we loved God, but that He loved us" (1 John 4:10). "Love the Lord your God with all your heart and love your neighbor as yourself" (Luke 10:27).

As the church of Jesus Christ we proclaim the gospel of love. That's why we exist. And we live among each other with such love and happiness and peace as to underline that truth.